Praise for Allen Klein, the world's only Jollytologist®, and his books

"I am always looking for ideas that help people enrich their lives. This book does just that. I highly recommend you read it and embrace its wise, and sometimes witty, words. They will feed your soul, lift your spirits, and help you live a fuller, richer, and more joy-filled life."

—SARK (Susan Ariel Rainbow Kennedy),
author of *Living Juicy*

"Allen Klein has a way of authentically bringing the gift of humor to every aspect of life. Yes, let laughter and a sense of humor bloom where you are planted and watch the joy you bring to yourself and others. Don't just buy this book—live it!"

—Terry Paulson,
PhD, author of *The Optimism Advantage*

"Allen Klein's purpose is to make us feel inspired again, to bask in laughter and revel in joy."

—*OM Times*

"If you are hungry for more joy in your life, then this is a must-have book. Open it to any page and allow good cheer to embrace you from the inside out."

—Susyn Reeve,
author of *The Inspired Life*

"The beauty in Allen Klein's work is clear. Regardless of the situations that life throws at us, Allen teaches and gently reminds us to laugh loudly, love passionately, and live our lives joyfully. Let Allen inspire you and help you embrace and celebrate the joy in your life and in the life that surrounds you."

—Carole Brody Fleet,
author of *Happily Even After*

"Words to live by are just words, unless you actually live by them. Take these words and love them—take these words and LIVE them!"

—BJ Gallagher,
author of *It's Never Too Late to Be What You Might Have Been*

"The world's only Jollytologist® is the one I turn to when I need jollying. I love that Allen Klein got into the business of joy when he learned the healing power of humor and has been on the case ever since."

—Nina Lesowitz,
co-author of *Living Life as a Thank You*

"Allen Klein is a noble and vital force watching over the human condition."

—Jerry Lewis

"I use quotations in all my books and presentations. A funny, profound, inspiring quote is a quick way to spice up material. Allen's collection is a great place to find some never-before-seen quotes that will make your communication more intriguing. Read it and reap."

—Sam Horn,
author of *POP!: Create the Perfect Pitch,*
Title and Tagline for Anything

"With a season of graduations and weddings ahead, not to mention anniversaries and forgotten birthdays, it'd be smart to have several copies of this book on hand. There is nothing not to like about it. But as marketable as the text is for gift-giving, it's also a great idea to keep your own copy for lonely times. Flipping through it at the beginning or end of each day can give you a little boost."

—Psych Central

always look
on the
bright side

Other Viva Editions books
by Allen Klein:

The Art of Living Joyfully:
How to be Happier Every Day of the Year

Change Your Life!:
A Little Book of Big Ideas

Inspiration for a Lifetime:
Words of Wisdom, Delight and Possibility

Mom's the Word:
The Wit, Wisdom and Wonder of Motherhood

Words of Love:
Quotations from the Heart

always look on the bright side

celebrating each day to the fullest

COMPILED BY
ALLEN KLEIN

FOREWORD BY
STEVE RIZZO

VIVA
EDITIONS

Published in the United States by Viva Editions, an imprint of Cleis Press, Inc., 2246 Sixth Street, Berkeley, California 94710.

Printed in South Korea.
Cover design: Scott Idleman/Blink
Cover photograph: Vasiliki Varvaki/Getty Images
Text design: Frank Wiedemann

First Edition.
10 9 8 7 6 5 4 3 2 1

Trade paper ISBN: 978-1-936740-55-0
E-book ISBN: 978-1-936740-64-2

Library of Congress Cataloging-in-Publication Data

Always look on the bright side : celebrating each day to the fullest / [compiles by] Allen Klein ; foreword by Steve Rizzo. -- FIRST EDITION.
    pages cm
 Includes index.
 ISBN 978-1-936740-55-0 (pbk. : alk. paper)
1. Conduct of life--Quotations, maxims, etc. 2. Life--Quotations, maxims, etc. I. Klein, Allen.
 PN6084.L53A49 2013
 081--dc23
                            2013022402

To my darling daughter Sarah,
who has continually shown me
the bright side of life.

Contents

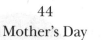

We're living in a world that's moving incredibly fast. On top of our personal problems and everyday pressures, the newspapers and evening newscasts tell us that our economy is falling apart, corporations are being forced to downsize and massive technological advances are causing people to re-evaluate, adjust and change their lives. Cell phones, Blackberries, iPhones and tablet devices, e-mails, text messages and even micro-communication applications like Twitter are clogging our minds with an overwhelming amount of information, leaving us with little or no time to relax, unwind and focus our attention on the big picture.

Hold on a second. I'm sorry, but I have to take a break here. I believe I'm getting depressed. I'll be right back.

Okay, I'm back now. Where was I? Oh yeah, I remember. Work harder, do more, get more, escape through television and movies, follow fitness and health programs that are meant to relax us but more often than not make us feel like we're adding one more task to our overcrowded schedules. It's really no wonder why so many of us have to be medicated in some way or another in order to cope with the madness our civilization has created!

We all need ways to reduce the tension, and deal with the fast pace that we are subjected to every day. In order to survive the insanity, we must occasionally step away from the world when it is too much with us and allow ourselves to experience a sacred time-out to nourish our souls. I honestly believe that this wonderful book does just that.

Always Look on the Bright Side is the essence of Allen Klein's thinking. As I read through it I was reminded of how powerful words can be. The quotations in this book will stir your emotions and spark your imagination. Some will take you back to precious moments from days gone by; others will cause you to reminisce and appreciate how important the simple things in life are.

The true beauty of this book, however, is that you can pick it up at any time, turn to any page and read any quote and you will feel something resonate within you. This book is a gem in that it reminds you that every day is a reason to rejoice and be thankful, regardless of your circumstance. It's an emotional roller coaster that embraces life to the fullest.

Here's the bottom line: I love this book simply because it has the power to make me feel good about myself and about life. I smiled, I laughed and at times I felt a tear or two roll down my cheek at the truth and wisdom that it contains. I believe you will do the same.

Steve Rizzo
Author of *Get Your SHIFT Together*

INTRODUCTION

In the movie *Monty Python's Life of Brian,* and later in the Broadway musical *Spamalot,* we are advised, with a light-hearted song, to "always look on the bright side of life." More recently, at the closing ceremony for the 2012 Summer Olympics in London, England, an estimated 750 million people watched as the composer of the song, Eric Idle, sang it accompanied by, among other things, nuns on roller skates, Roman soldiers and Indian Bollywood dancers.

Behind this seemingly frivolous and cheerful tune is perhaps a deeper message telling us that we have a choice about how we view life's experiences. It is always up to us whether we look on the bright side or the dark side.

Whether we see the glass as half-full or half-empty, whether we let someone else's gloomy outlook drag us down, whether we choose to have a great day or not, is a matter of choice. Every millisecond of the day, whether we realize it or not, we are deciding to be positive or negative about what life has handed us.

I'm a firm believer in the power of words to change our life. Whether it be in the form of affirmations, prayers or quotations, words can encourage us to do what all those folks at the Olympics were singing about...to always look on the bright side of life.

We usually remember to celebrate a birthday, a holiday or a special anniversary. But we frequently forget that every day is special and a time to celebrate.

We can celebrate the glory of the sun rising, a spectacular sunset, a heavy rain or a snow-covered field. We can celebrate the beauty of a flower, the smile of a child or the song of a bird. But we need also not to forget to celebrate and honor the work we do, our own unique gifts or the special people in our lives.

This book can help you do all of that. It is filled with quotations to help you not only celebrate special occasions but rejoice every day as well. Even the smallest moments in life are cause for a celebration...from the clarity of a perfect autumn day to the challenge of changing a diaper.

There is no shortage of things to delight in and embrace in this world.

On the following pages, you have over 500 quotations on the marvels of life, from the famous to the anonymous. Sometimes heartwarming, sometimes humorous, always insightful and uplifting, these quotes are the perfect pick-me-ups for you or for sharing with others.

I hope that the wise, witty and perceptive words in this book help inspire you to live your life to the fullest, to make every day a special day and to always look on the bright side of life.

Allen Klein
San Francisco, California

The more you praise and
celebrate your life,
the more there is in life to
celebrate.

O P R A H   W I N F R E Y

Celebrate
Today

Write it on your heart that every day is
the best day of the year.

RALPH WALDO EMERSON

Like fireworks, this universe is a celebration and you are
the spectator contemplating the eternal Fourth of July
of your absolute splendor.

FRANCIS LUCILLE

Greet each day with your eyes open to beauty,
your mind open to change, and your heart open to love.

PAULA FINN

Live each day as if your life
had just begun.

JOHANN WOLFGANG
VON GOETHE

We live in a wonderful world that is full of beauty,
charm and adventure. There is no end to the adventures
that we can have if only we seek them with our eyes open.

JAWAHARLAL NEHRU

Live your life each day, as you would climb a mountain.
An occasional glance towards the summit
keeps the goal in mind,
but many beautiful scenes are to be observed
from each new vantage point.

HAROLD B. MELCHART

Every day is a good day.

YUN-MEN

Stop worrying about the potholes in the road
and celebrate the journey!

BARBARA HOFFMAN

The only way to live is to accept each minute
as an unrepeatable miracle, which is exactly what it is:
a miracle and unrepeatable.

STORM JAMESON

Look, I really don't want to wax philosophical, but I will say that if you're alive, you got to flap your arms and legs, you got to jump around a lot, you got to make a lot of noise, because life is the very opposite of death. And therefore, as I see it, if you're quiet, you're not living. You've got to be noisy, or at least your thoughts should be noisy and colorful and lively.

MEL BROOKS

Morning is when I am awake and there is a dawn in me.

HENRY DAVID THOREAU

Each day of your life, as soon as you open your eyes in the morning, you can square away for a happy and successful day.

GEORGE MATTHEW ADAMS

It is completely usual for me to get up in the morning, take a look around, and laugh out loud.

BARBARA KINGSOLVER

Today, this hour, this minute is the day, the hour, the minute for each of us to sense the fact that life is good, with all its trials and troubles, and perhaps more interesting because of them.

ROBERT UPDEGRAFF

Don't judge each day by the harvest you reap, but by the seeds you plant.

ROBERT LOUIS STEVENSON

Today a thousand doors of enterprise are open to you, inviting you to useful work.
To live at this time is an inestimable privilege, and a sacred obligation devolves upon you to make right use of your opportunities. Today is the day in which to attempt and achieve something worthwhile.

GRENVILLE KLEISER

Try to make at least one person happy every day,
and then in ten years you may have made three
thousand, six hundred and fifty persons happy, or
brightened a small town by your contribution to the
fund of general enjoyment.

SYDNEY SMITH

Wherever you go, no matter what the weather,
always bring your own sunshine.

ANTHONY J. D'ANGELO

So never let a cloudy day ruin your sunshine,
for even if you can't see it, the sunshine is still there,
inside of you ready to shine when you will let it.

AMY PITZELE

When you wake up in the morning, you must really wake
up totally—physically and mentally.
Otherwise, don't bother with the day.

CHUNGLIANG AL HUANG

Nothing should be more highly prized
than the value of each day.

JOHANN WOLFGANG VON GOETHE

Have fun. I don't kid myself.
Life is very fragile, and success doesn't change that. If
anything, success makes it more fragile.
Anything can change, without warning, and that's why I
try not to take any of what's happened too seriously.

DONALD TRUMP

If you are not playful you are not alive.

DAVID HOCKNEY

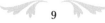

I don't want to get to the end
of my life and find that I have
just lived the length of it.
I want to have lived the width
of it as well.

DIANE ACKERMAN

Jump into the middle of things, get your hands dirty,
fall flat on your face, and then reach for the stars.

JOAN L. CURCIO

Why not go out on a limb? Isn't that where the fruit is?

FRANK SCULLY

The only way to have a life is to commit to it like crazy.

ANGELINA JOLIE

If you obey all the rules you miss all the fun.

KATHARINE HEPBURN

Life leaps like a geyser for those willing
to drill through the rock of inertia.

ALEXIS CARREL

If your ship doesn't come in, swim out to it!

JONATHAN WINTERS

A ship in harbor is safe—
but that is not what ships are built for.

JOHN A. SHEDD

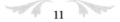

11

When you're skating on thin ice,
you may as well tap-dance.

BRYCE COURTENAY

Skating on thin ice is better than skating on no ice at all.

JOHN M. SHANAHAN

Instead of seeing the rug being pulled from under us,
we can learn to dance on a shifting carpet.

THOMAS CRUM

The only way to make sense out of change is
to plunge into it, move with it, and join the dance.

ALAN W. WATTS

Let that day be lost to us
on which we did not dance once!

FRIEDRICH NIETZSCHE

Live as you will have wished to have lived
when you are dying.

CHRISTIAN FÜRCHTEGOTT GELLERT

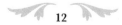

Time is the coin of your life. It is the only coin you have,
and only you can determine how it will be spent.
Be careful lest you let other people spend it for you.

CARL SANDBURG

When making your choice in life, do not neglect to live.

SAMUEL JOHNSON

One of the most tragic things I know about human
nature is that all of us tend to put off living.
We are all dreaming of some magical
rose garden over the horizon—
instead of enjoying the roses
blooming outside our windows today.

DALE CARNEGIE

Do not look back on happiness
or dream of it in the future.
You are only sure of today;
do not let yourself be cheated out of it.

HENRY WARD BEECHER

Grab a chance
and you won't be sorry for a might-have-been.
ARTHUR MICHELL RANSOME

When the days are too short
chances are you are living at your best.
EARL NIGHTINGALE

The whole world is an art gallery when you're mindful.
There are beautiful things everywhere—and they're free.
CHARLES TART

The world is its own magic.
SHUNRYU SUZUKI

Normal day, let me be aware of the treasure you are.
MARY JEAN IRION

There is no such thing in anyone's life
as an unimportant day.
ALEXANDER WOOLLCOTT

Sooner or later we all discover that the important moments in life are not the advertised ones, not the birthdays, the graduations, the weddings, not the great goals achieved. The real milestones are less prepossessing. They come to the door of memory unannounced, stray dogs that amble in, sniff around a bit and simply never leave. Our lives are measured by these.

SUSAN B. ANTHONY

Stop sitting there with your hands folded, looking on, doing nothing: Get into action and live this full and glorious life NOW. You have to do it.

EILEEN CADDY

If we are ever to enjoy life, now is the time, not tomorrow or next year...
Today should always be our most wonderful day.

THOMAS DREIER

I live now and only now, and I will do what I want to do this moment and not what I decided was best for me yesterday.

HUGH PRATHER

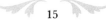

Yesterday is ashes;
tomorrow wood.
Only today
does the fire burn brightly.

ESKIMO SAYING

Never again clutter your days or nights with so many
menial and unimportant things that you have no time to
accept a real challenge when it comes along. This applies
to play as well as work. A day merely survived is no cause
for celebration. You are not here to fritter away your
precious hours when you have the ability to accomplish
so much by making a slight change in your routine.
No more busy work. No more hiding from success. Leave
time, leave space, to grow. Now. Now! Not tomorrow!

OG MANDINO

It is only possible to live happily ever after
on a day-to-day basis.

MARGARET BONANNO

The past is behind, learn from it;
The future is ahead, prepare for it;
The present is here, live it.

THOMAS MONSON

Take the reins of your life in your hands every day. Get
up and put a smile on your face, and feel grateful for this
gift that is your life.

SUSAN L. TAYLOR

Each day comes bearing its own gifts. Untie the ribbons.

RUTH ANN SCHABACKER

I live a day at a time.
Each day I look for a kernel of excitement.
In the morning, I say:
"What is my exciting thing for today?"
Then, I do the day. Don't ask me about tomorrow.

BARBARA JORDAN

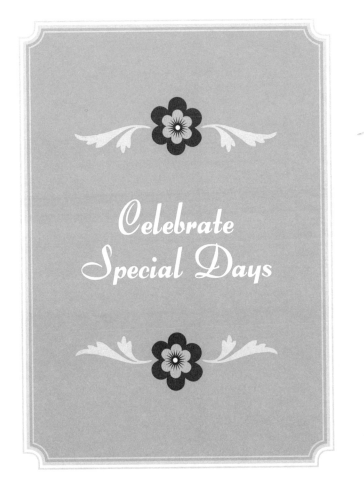

Celebrate
Special Days

Birthdays

There was a star danced, and under that was I born.

WILLIAM SHAKESPEARE

Our birthdays are feathers in the broad wing of time.

JEAN PAUL RICHTER

Because time itself is like a spiral,
something special happens
on your birthday each year:
The same energy that God invested
in you at birth is present once again.

MENACHEM MENDEL SCHNEERSON

Most of us can remember a time when a birthday—
especially if it was ones' own—
brightened the world as if a second sun had risen.

ROBERT LYND

Birthdays are good for you.
The more you have, the longer you live.

ANONYMOUS

A birthday is just the first day of another 365-day journey
around the sun. Enjoy the trip!

ANONYMOUS

I'm six foot eleven. My birthday covers three days.

DARRYL DAWKINS

Born of a Monday, fair in the face,
Born of a Tuesday, full of God's grace,
Born of a Wednesday, merry and glad,
Born of a Thursday, sour and sad,
Born of a Friday, Godly given,
Born of a Saturday, work for your living.
Born of a Sunday, ne'er shall you want,
So ends the week, and there's an end on't.

ANONYMOUS

For all the advances in medicine,
there is still no cure for the common birthday.

JOHN GLENN

Birth may be a matter of a moment,
but it is a unique one.

FREDERICK LEBOYER

Do not despair, every new born baby is a potential prophet.

R. D. Laing

We are all born naked and screaming and if you're lucky
that sort of thing won't stop there.

ANONYMOUS

Middle Age:
Later than you think and sooner than you expect.

EARL WILSON

Middle age is when your age starts to show
around your middle.

BOB HOPE

The last birthday that's any good is 23.

ANDY ROONEY

You know how you tell when you're getting old?
When your broad mind changes places
with your narrow waist.

RED SKELTON

I have everything now I had twenty years ago—
except now it's all lower.

GYPSY ROSE LEE

At thirty, a body has a mind of its own.

BETTE MIDLER

Fifty years old, 212 fights, and I'm still pretty.

MUHAMMAD ALI

At age fifty, every man has the face he deserves.

GEORGE ORWELL

One starts to get young at the age of sixty.

PABLO PICASSO

My parents didn't want to move to Florida,
but they turned sixty, and it was the law.

JERRY SEINFELD

Retire? That's ridiculous.
What does it for you is to have something to get up for in
the morning. Now, they say, you should retire at seventy.
When I was seventy, I still had pimples.

GEORGE BURNS

There is a fountain of youth: It is your mind, your talents, the creativity you bring to your life and the lives of the people you love. When you learn to tap this source, you will have truly defeated age.

SOPHIA LOREN

Whatever a man's age may be, he can reduce it several years by putting a bright-colored flower in his buttonhole.

MARK TWAIN

One advantage in growing older is that you can stand for more and fall for less.

MONTA CRANE

I'd like to grow very old as slowly as possible.

IRENE MAYER SELZNICK

The secret of staying young is to live honestly, eat slowly, and lie about your age.

LUCILLE BALL

Age is a number and mine is unlisted.

ANONYMOUS

Live your life and forget your age.

FRANK BERING

Youth is the gift of nature, but age is a work of art.

GARSON KANIN

How old would you be
if you didn't know how old you are?

SATCHEL PAIGE

We are always the same age inside.

GERTRUDE STEIN

If you carry your childhood with you,
you never become older.

ABRAHAM SUTZKEVER

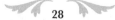

I don't know what the big deal
is about old age.
Old people who shine
from inside look
ten to twenty years younger.

DOLLY PARTON

"Don't worry about senility," my grandfather used to say.
"When it hits you, you won't know it."

BILL COSBY

A man ninety years old was asked to what he attributed
his longevity. I reckon, he said, with a twinkle in his eye,
it's because most nights I went to bed and slept when I
should have sat up and worried.

DOROTHEA KENT

Old age is not so bad when you consider the alternatives.

MAURICE CHEVALIER

Old age is when the liver spots show through your gloves.

PHYLLIS DILLER

If you survive long enough, you're revered—
rather like an old building.

KATHARINE HEPBURN

When I was young, the Dead Sea was still alive.

GEORGE BURNS

He who is of a calm and happy nature
will hardly feel the pressure of age.

PLATO

Sometimes, when I realize I am 101 years old, it hits me
right between the eyes. I say, "Oh Lord, how did this
happen?" Turning one hundred was the worst birthday
of my life. I wouldn't wish it on my worst enemy. Turning
101 was not so bad. Once you're past that century mark,
it's just not as shocking.

BESSIE DELANY

You're not getting older, you're getting better.

ANONYMOUS

And in the end it's not the years in your life that count.
It's the life in your years.

ABRAHAM LINCOLN

May all your future years be
Free from disappointment, care or strife,
That every birthday you will be
A little more in love with life.

ANONYMOUS

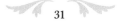

New Year's Day

Cheers to a new year and another chance
for us to get it right.

OPRAH WINFREY

New Year's Day is special only
as a symbol of a new beginning.
The realty is that every day is a new beginning,
a new chance to create the life that we desire.

KEVIN EIKENBERRY

In the New Year, may your right hand always
be stretched out in friendship, but never in want.

IRISH TOAST

Valentine's Day

In the coldest February, as in every other month in every other year, the best thing to hold on to in this world is each other.

LINDA ELLERBEE

One of the oldest human needs is having someone to wonder where you are when you don't come home at night.

MARGARET MEAD

In love the paradox occurs that two beings become one and yet remain two.

ERICH FROMM

Love is composed of a single soul inhabiting two bodies.

ARISTOTLE

For it was not into my ear you whispered, but into my heart. It was not my lips you kissed, but my soul.

JUDY GARLAND

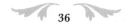

Love is to the heart
what the summer is to the farmer's year.
It brings to harvest all the loveliest flowers of the soul.

BILLY GRAHAM

Sometimes the heart sees what is invisible to the eye.

H. JACKSON BROWN, JR.

Love is like an hourglass, with the heart filling up
as the brain empties.

JULES RENARD

The heart knows things that the mind will never know.

CARL HAMMERSCHLAG

The moment you have in your heart this extraordinary
thing called love and feel the depth, the delight, the
ecstasy of it, you will discover that for you the world is
transformed.

J. KRISHNAMURTI

Love doesn't make
the world go round.
Love is what makes
the ride worthwhile.

FRANKLIN P. JONES

Treasure the love you receive above all.
It will survive long after your good health has vanished.

OG MANDINO

What the world really needs is
more love and less paperwork.

PEARL BAILEY

The cure for all ills and wrongs, the cares, the sorrows
and the crimes of humanity, all lie in the one word "love."
It is the divine vitality that everywhere produces and
restores life.

LYDIA MARIA CHILD

Love is the immortal flow of energy that nourishes,
extends and preserves. Its eternal goal is life.

SMILEY BLANTON

Where there is love there is life.

MAHATMA GANDHI

Life without love is like a tree without blossoms or fruit.

KAHLIL GIBRAN

We are all born for love.
It is the principle of existence, and its only end.

BENJAMIN DISRAELI

The supreme happiness in life is the conviction
that we are loved.

VICTOR HUGO

Being deeply loved by someone gives you strength;
loving someone deeply gives you courage.

LAO-TZU

Love conquers all things except poverty and a toothache.

MAE WEST

It was always the power of love that pulled us through.
And it was the power of laughter
that kept us from falling apart.

STEVE RIZZO

You were born together, and together you shall be forev-
ermore.… But let there be spaces in your togetherness.
And let the winds of the heavens dance between you.

KAHLIL GIBRAN

If you love somebody, let them go. If they return,
they were always yours. If they don't, they never were.

ANONYMOUS

A lady of forty-seven who has been married twenty-seven
years and has six children knows what love really is and
once described it for me like this: "Love is what you've
been through with somebody."

JAMES THURBER

Love means never having to say you're sorry.

ERICH SEGAL

Love is an act of endless forgiveness,
a tender look which becomes a habit.

PETER USTINOV

Perfect love is rare indeed—for to be a lover will require
that you continually have the subtlety of the very wise,
the flexibility of the child, the sensitivity of the artist, the
understanding of the philosopher, the acceptance of the
saint, the tolerance of the scholar and the fortitude of
the certain.

LEO BUSCAGLIA

Love is not counting the years;
it's making the years count.

ANONYMOUS

Love has nothing to do with
what you are expecting to get,
it's what you are expected to give—which is everything.

ANONYMOUS

You will find as you look back upon your life
that the moments when you have truly lived
are the moments when you have done things
in the spirit of love.

HENRY DRUMMOND

Those who love deeply never grow old;
they may die of old age, but they die young.

SIR ARTHUR WING PINERO

Do all things with love.

Og Mandino

Mother's Day

God could not be everywhere,
and therefore he created mothers.

JEWISH PROVERB

The hand that rocks the cradle
Is the hand that rules the world.

WILLIAM ROSS WALLACE

The mother is the most precious possession of the nation,
so precious that society advances its highest well-being
when it protects the functions of the mother.

ELLEN KEY

Most of all the other beautiful things in life come by twos
and threes, by dozens and hundreds. Plenty of roses,
stars, sunsets, rainbows, brothers and sisters, aunts and
cousins, but only one mother in the whole world.

KATE DOUGLAS WIGGIN

A mother is she who can take the place of all others
but whose place no one else can take.

CARDINAL GASPARD MERMILLOD

I think my life began with waking up
and loving my mother's face.

GEORGE ELIOT

The three most beautiful sights:
a potato garden in bloom, a ship in sail,
a woman after the birth of her child.

IRISH PROVERB

Motherhood is a wonderful thing—
what a pity to waste it on children.

JUDITH PUGH

Motherhood: All love begins and ends here.

ROBERT BROWNING

I was not a classic mother. But my kids were never
palmed off to boarding school. So, I didn't bake cookies.
You can buy cookies, but you can't buy love.

RAQUEL WELCH

A mother is a person who, seeing there are only four
pieces of pie for five people, promptly announces she
never did care for pie.

TENNEVA JORDAN

What my mother believed about cooking is that if you
worked hard and prospered,
someone else would do it for you.

NORA EPHRON

I come from a Greek household. My mother wouldn't let
the FedEx man come in without eating.

ARIANNA HUFFINGTON

My mother's menu consisted of two choices:
Take it or leave it.

BUDDY HACKETT

Food, love, career, and mothers,
the four major guilt groups.

CATHY GUISEWITE

Mothers have big aprons—
to cover the faults of their children.

JEWISH SAYING

The commonest fallacy among women is that simply
having children makes one a mother—which is as absurd
as believing that having a piano makes one a musician.

SYDNEY J. HARRIS

There is no such thing as a non-working mother.

HESTER MUNDIS

"Working mother" is a misnomer.… It implies that
any mother without a definite career is indolently not
working, lolling around eating bon-bons, reading novels,
and watching soap operas. But the word "mother"
is already a synonym for some of the hardest, most
demanding work ever shouldered by any human.

LIZ SMITH

Any mother could perform the jobs
of several air-traffic controllers with ease.

LISA ALTHER

Motherhood is not for the fainthearted. Frogs, skinned knees, and the insults of teenage girls are not meant for the wimpy.

DANIELLE STEEL

A suburban mother's role is to deliver children obstetrically once, and by car forever after.

PETER DE VRIES

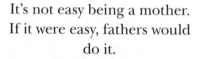

It's not easy being a mother.
If it were easy, fathers would
do it.

DOROTHY, ON
THE GOLDEN GIRLS

What do you get on Mother's Day if you have kids?
You know what. A card with flowers that are made out
of pink toilet paper—a lot of pink toilet paper. You get
breakfast in bed. Then you get up and fix everybody else
their breakfast. And then you go to the bathroom, and
you are out of toilet paper.

LIZ SCOTT

Romance fails us and so do friendships,
but the relationship of mother and child remains
indelible and indestructible—
the strongest bond on earth.

THEODOR REIK

Youth fades, love droops, the leaves of friendship fall;
A mother's secret hope outlives them all.

OLIVER WENDELL HOLMES

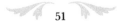

A mother is the truest friend we have, when trials heavy
and sudden, fall upon us; when adversity takes the place
of prosperity; when friends who rejoice with us in our
sunshine desert us; when trouble thickens around us; still
will she cling to us and endeavor by her kind precepts
and counsels to dissipate the clouds of darkness and
cause peace to return to our hearts.

WASHINGTON IRVING

The heart of a mother is a deep abyss at the bottom of
which you will always find forgiveness.

HONORÉ DE BALZAC

The mother's heart is the child's schoolroom.

HENRY WARD BEECHER

Mother is the name for God in the lips
and hearts of little children.

WILLIAM MAKEPEACE THACKERAY

A mother understands what a child does not say.

SAYING

No matter how old a mother is she watches her
middle-aged children for signs of improvement.

FLORIDA SCOTT-MAXWELL

Mama exhorted her children at every opportunity
to "jump at de sun." We might not land on the sun,
but at least we would get off the ground.

ZORA NEALE HURSTON

I have a last thank-you. It is to my mother Celia Amster
Bader, the bravest and strongest person I have known,
who was taken from me much too soon. I pray that I may
be all that she would have been had she lived in an age
when women could aspire and achieve and daughters are
cherished as much as sons.

RUTH BADER GINSBURG

Mama seemed to do only what my father wanted,
and yet we lived the way my mother wanted us to live.

LILLIAN HELLMAN

Men are what their mothers made them.

RALPH WALDO EMERSON

There was never a great man who had not a great mother.

OLIVER SCHREINER

All that I am, or hope to be, I owe to my angel mother.

ABRAHAM LINCOLN

Mother knows best.

EDNA FERBER

Father's Day—when a man who is proud of his family
finds his family is proud of him.

ANONYMOUS

Father's Day is like Mother's Day,
except the gift is cheaper.

GERALD F. LIEBERMAN

Fatherhood is pretending the present you love most
is soap-on-a-rope.

BILL COSBY

Blessed indeed is the man
who hears many gentle voices call him father!

LYDIA MARIA CHILD

It is much easier to become a father than to be one.

KENT NERBURN

Any man can be a father,
but it takes someone special to be a dad.

ANNE GEDDES

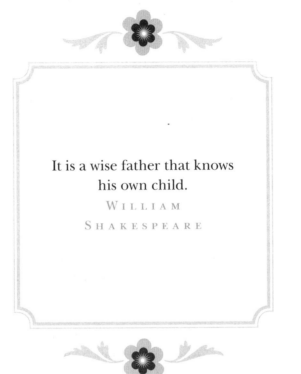

It is a wise father that knows
his own child.

WILLIAM

SHAKESPEARE

To be a successful father there's one absolute rule:
When you have a kid,
don't look at it for the first two years.

ERNEST HEMINGWAY

Everybody knows that fatherhood reveals your limitations. But less well known is that, now and then, fatherhood also brings out skills that might well have gone undiscovered were it not for having kids.

HUGH O'NEILL

A man finds out what is meant by a spitting image
when he tries to feed cereal to his infant.

IMOGENE FEY

Show me a man who has no fear
and I'll show you a man who's never changed a diaper.

W. H. MERTZ III

It doesn't matter who my father was;
it matters who I remember he was.

ANNE SEXTON

Spread the diaper in the position of the diamond with
you at bat. Then fold second base down to home and
set the baby on the pitcher's mound. Put first base and
third together, bring up home plate and pin the three
together. Of course, in case of rain,
you gotta call the game and start all over again.

JIMMY PIERSALL

A baby has a way of making a man out of his father
and a boy out of his grandfather.

ANGIE PAPADAKIS

A father is always making his baby into a little woman.
And when she is a woman he turns her back again.

ENID BAGNOLD

She got her good looks from her father.
He's a plastic surgeon.

GROUCHO MARX

Old as she was, she still missed her daddy sometimes.

GLORIA NAYLOR

Directly after God in heaven comes Papa.

WOLFGANG AMADEUS MOZART

There's something like a line of gold thread running through a man's words when he talks to his daughter, and gradually over the years it gets to be long enough for you to pick up in your hands and weave into a cloth that feels like love itself.

JOHN GREGORY BROWN

It is admirable for a man to take his son fishing, but there is a special place in heaven for the father who takes his daughter shopping.

JOHN SINOR

The most important thing a father can do for his children is to love their mother.

THEODORE M. HESBURGH

You don't have to deserve your mother's love. You have to deserve your father's. He's more particular.

ROBERT FROST

A good father is a little bit of a mother.

LEE SALK

The affection of a father and a son are different: The father loves the person of the son, and the son loves the memory of his father.

ANONYMOUS

What you have inherited from your father, you must earn over again for yourselves, or it will not be yours.

JOHANN WOLFGANG VON GOETHE

My father used to play with my brother and me in the yard. Mother would come out and say, "You're tearing up the grass." "We're not raising grass," Dad would reply. "We're raising boys."

HARMON KILLEBREW

My father gave me the greatest gift anyone could give another person, he believed in me.

JIM VALVANO

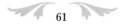

By the time a man realizes that maybe his father was
right, he usually has a son who thinks he's wrong.

CHARLES WADSWORTH

A father decided to tell his young son the facts of life and
was stumped right away by the boy's first question:
"How many are there?"

ANONYMOUS

It is not flesh and blood but the heart
which makes us fathers and sons.

JOHANN SCHILLER

I would say one thing to any father listening: Genuinely
express love to your son, to your daughter. It's better
to take the risk that it won't be heard, or that it will be
thrown back in your face, than not to do it.

MICHAEL MEADE

If there is any immortality to be had among us human
beings, it is certainly only in the love that we leave
behind. Fathers like mine don't ever die.

LEO BUSCAGLIA

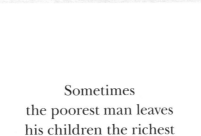

Sometimes
the poorest man leaves
his children the richest
inheritance.

RUTH E. RENKEL

When I was a boy of fourteen, my father was so ignorant
I could hardly stand to have the old man around.
But when I got to be twenty-one, I was astonished
at how much he had learned in seven years.

MARK TWAIN

You know, fathers just have a way
of putting everything together.

ERIKA COSBY

Sherman made the terrible discovery that men make
about their fathers sooner or later...that the man before
him was not an aging father but a boy, a boy much like
himself, a boy who grew up and had a child of his own
and, as best he could, out of a sense of duty and, perhaps
love, adopted a role called Being a Father so that his
child would have something mythical and infinitely
important: a Protector, who would keep a lid on all the
chaotic and catastrophic possibilities of life.

TOM WOLFE

I cannot think of any need in childhood as strong
as the need for a father's protection.

SIGMUND FREUD

There are three stages in a man's life: "My Daddy can
whip your Daddy." "Aw, Dad, you don't know anything."
"My father used to say…."

DWIGHT MCSMITH

My father never raised his hand
to any one of his children,
except in self-defense.

FRED ALLEN

Life was a lot simpler when what we honored was father
and mother rather than all major credit cards.

ROBERT ORBEN

A father carries pictures where his money used to be.

ANONYMOUS

The words that a father speaks to his children in the
privacy of home are not heard by the world,
but, as in whispering galleries,
they are clearly heard at the end, and by posterity.

JEAN PAUL RICHTER

My father didn't tell me how to live;
he lived, and let me watch him do it.

CLARENCE BUDINGTON KELLAND

Manual labor to my father was not only good and decent
for its own sake, but as he was given to saying,
it straightened out one's thoughts.

MARY ELLEN CHASE

My father taught me to work;
he did not teach me to love it.
I never did like to work, and I don't deny it.
I'd rather read,
tell stories, crack jokes, talk, laugh—
anything but work.

ABRAHAM LINCOLN

I watched a small man with thick calluses on both hands
work fifteen and sixteen hours a day. I saw him once liter-
ally bleed from the bottoms of his feet, a man who came
here uneducated, alone, unable to speak the language,
who taught me all I needed to know about faith and hard
work by the simple eloquence of his example.

MARIO CUOMO (SPEAKING OF HIS FATHER)

My father taught me
that the only way you can make good at anything
is to practice, and then practice some more.

PETE ROSE

My father instilled in me
the attitude of prevailing. If
there's a challenge, go for it. If
there's a wall to break down,
break it down.

DONNY OSMOND

My father said:
"You must never try to make all the money
that's in a deal. Let the other fellow make some money
too, because if you have a reputation for always making
all the money, you won't have many deals."

J. PAUL GETTY

One father is more than a hundred schoolmasters.

GEORGE HERBERT

Father knows best.

SAYING

Graduation

Academe, n.: An ancient school where morality and philosophy were taught. Academy, n.: A modern school where football is taught.

AMBROSE BIERCE

A graduation ceremony is an event
where the commencement
speaker tells thousands of students
dressed in identical caps
and gowns that "individuality" is the key to success.

ROBERT ORBEN

Commencement speeches were invented
largely in the belief
that outgoing college students
should never be released into
the world until they have been properly sedated.

GARRY TRUDEAU

A professor is someone who talks in someone else's sleep.

W. H. AUDEN

Yes, the lectures are optional. Graduation is also optional.

BOB BICKFORD

"Commencement speakers," said Father Flynn,
"should think of themselves as the body
at an old-fashioned Irish wake.
They need you in order to have the party,
but nobody expects you to say very much."

MARIO CUOMO

My father gave me these hints on speech-making:
"Be sincere...be brief...be seated."

JAMES ROOSEVELT

There is a good reason they call these ceremonies
"commencement exercises." Graduation is not the end;
it's the beginning.

ORRIN HATCH

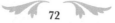

You are educated. Your certification is in your degree.
You may think of it as the ticket to the good life. Let me
ask you to think of an alternative. Think of it as your
ticket to change the world.

TOM BROKAW

You cannot help but learn more as you take the world
into your hands. Take it up reverently, for it is an old
piece of clay, with millions of thumbprints on it.

JOHN UPDIKE

You hold all our futures in
your hands. So you better
make it good.

JODIE FOSTER

As you take leave of [your school],
as you graduate into a new life of
the mind, may each of you ask yourself this:
What am I doing to
increase the sum hope of the world?
What am I doing to teach
someone else what I have learned?

ARTHUR BURNS

Education should be a lifelong process,
the formal period serving as a foundation on which life's
structure may rest and rise.

ROBERT H. JACKSON

Education is what survives when what has been learned
has been forgotten.

B. F. SKINNER

You're college graduates now, so use your education.
Remember: It's not who you know, it's whom.

JOAN RIVERS

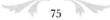

The aim of all education is, or should be,
to teach people to educate themselves.

ARNOLD J. TOYNBEE

A university education should equip one
to entertain three things:
a friend, an idea and one's self.

THOMAS EHRLICH

Education is learning
what you didn't even know you didn't know.

DANIEL J. BOORSTIN

My grandmother wanted me to have an education,
so she kept me out of school.

MARGARET MEAD

Your families are extremely proud of you.
You can't imagine the sense of relief
they are experiencing.
This would be a most opportune time to ask for money.

GARY BOLDING

If you think education is expensive, try ignorance!

DEREK BOK

Study hard, and you might grow up to be President. But let's face it: Even then, you'll never make as much money as your dog.

GEORGE BUSH

(AFTER LEARNING MILLIE, HIS DOG,
MADE ALMOST $900,000 IN BOOK ROYALTIES)

[Public school graduates] go forth…
into a world of whose
richness and subtlety they have no conception.
They go forth
into it with well-developed bodies, fairly developed
minds, and underdeveloped hearts.

E. M. FORSTER

Just about a month from now I'm set adrift,
with a diploma for a sail and lots of nerve for oars.

RICHARD HALLIBURTON

Have interesting failures.... If you need to have a personal crisis have it now. Don't wait until midlife, when it will take longer to resolve.... Don't pity yourselves. Lighten up. Seek people with a sense of humor. Avoid humorless people— and do not marry one, for God's sake.

GARRISON KEILLOR
(COMMENCEMENT ADDRESS ADVICE)

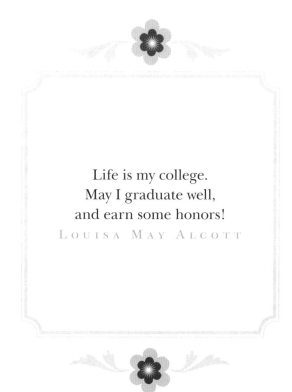

Life is my college.
May I graduate well,
and earn some honors!

LOUISA MAY ALCOTT

Never become so much of an expert that you stop gaining expertise. View life as a continuous learning experience.

DENIS WAITLEY

There is no more beautiful life than that of a student.

F. ALBRECHT

Each day grow older, and learn something new.

SOLON

The trouble with learning from experience is that you never graduate.

DOUG LARSON

It is indeed ironic that we spend our school days yearning to graduate and our remaining days waxing nostalgic about our school days.

ISABEL WAXMAN

Thanksgiving

Thanksgiving is so called because
we are all so thankful that it only comes once a year.

P. J. O'ROURKE

Nine-tenths of wisdom is appreciation. Go find somebody's hand and squeeze it, while there's time.

DALE DAUTEN

As we express our gratitude, we must never forget that
the highest appreciation is not to utter words, but to live
by them.

JOHN FITZGERALD KENNEDY

Courtesies of a small and trivial character
are the ones which strike deepest in the grateful
and appreciating heart.

HENRY CLAY

Let's be grateful for those who give us happiness; they
are the charming gardeners who make our souls bloom.

MARCEL PROUST

Sometimes our light goes out but is blown
into flame by another human being.
Each of us owes deepest thanks to those
who have rekindled this light.

ALBERT SCHWEITZER

Gratitude is one of the sweet shortcuts
to finding peace of mind and happiness inside.
No matter what's going on outside of us,
there's always something we could be grateful for.

BARRY NEIL KAUFMAN

Feeling gratitude and not expressing it
is like wrapping a present and not giving it.

WILLIAM ARTHUR WARD

Christmas

Christmas, children, is not a date. It is a state of mind.

MARY ELLEN CHASE

Christmas waves a magic wand over this world, and
behold, everything is softer and more beautiful.

NORMAN VINCENT PEALE

Christmas is the season for kindling the fire of hospitality
in the hall, the genial flame of charity in the heart.

WASHINGTON IRVING

I will honor Christmas in my heart,
and try to keep it all the year.

CHARLES DICKENS

From home to home, and heart to heart, from one place
to another. The warmth and joy of Christmas, brings us
closer to each other.

EMILY MATTHEWS

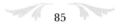

He who has no Christmas in his heart
will never find Christmas under a tree.

SUNSHINE MAGAZINE

Christmas—that magic blanket that wraps itself about us,
that something so intangible that it is like a fragrance.
It may weave a spell of nostalgia. Christmas may be a day
of feasting, or of prayer, but always it will be a day
of remembrance—a day in which we think of
everything we have ever loved.

AUGUSTA E. RUNDEL

Blessed is the season which engages
the whole world in a conspiracy of love.

HAMILTON WRIGHT MABIE

Selfishness makes Christmas a burden.
Love makes it a delight.

ANONYMOUS

There is no ideal Christmas;
only the one Christmas you decide
to make as a reflection of your values,
desires, affections, traditions.

BILL McKIBBEN

Until one feels the spirit of Christmas, there is no
Christmas. All else is outward display—so much tinsel
and decorations. For it isn't the holly, it isn't the snow.
It isn't the tree nor the firelight's glow. It's the warmth
that comes to the hearts of men when the Christmas
spirit returns again.

ANONYMOUS

A Christmas candle is a lovely thing; It makes no noise
at all, But softly gives itself away; While quite unselfish, it
grows small.

EVA K. LOGUE

I have often thought, it happens very well that
Christmas should fall in the Middle of Winter.

JOSEPH ADDISON

Perhaps the best Yuletide decoration
is being wreathed in smiles.

ANONYMOUS

What I don't like about office Christmas parties
is looking for a job the next day.

PHYLLIS DILLER

What do you call people who are afraid of Santa Claus?
Claustrophobic.

ANONYMOUS

Santa Claus has the right idea.
Visit people once a year.
VICTOR BORGE

Five things I've learned from Santa:
1- Dress in colorful clothing.
2- Lose the girdle.
3- See the world.
4- Let others do the heavy lifting.
5- Keep working, if only part time.
ANONYMOUS

Yes, Virginia, there is a Santa Claus.
He exists as certainly as love
and generosity and devotion exist.
FRANCIS P. CHURCH

Hanukkah

"Jewish Christmas"—that's what my gentile friends called
Chanukah when I was growing up in Michigan in the
thirties and forties.

FAYE MOSKOWITZ

You don't go to heder [Hebrew school] for eight days in a
row, you eat pancakes every day, spin your dreidel [four-
sided top] to your heart's content, and from all sides
Hanukkah money comes pouring in. What holiday could
be better than that?

SHOLEM ALEICHEM

On Hanukkah, the Jew is fully prepared to believe in
miracles. He retells the story of the tiny vessel of oil
which burned eight days and assures himself that when
a man has faith anything can happen—even Hanukkah
latkes [potato pancakes] in the jungle.

ZELDA POPKIN

We light candles in testament that faith
makes miracles possible.

NACHUM BRAVERMAN

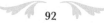

In the depth of winter, for eight straight evenings,
the entire family gathers to light candles of hope.

MORRIS N. KERTZER

The commandment to light the Hanukkah lamp is an
exceedingly precious one, and one should be particularly
careful to fulfill it, in order to make known the miracle,
and to offer additional praise...to God for the wonders
which He has wrought for us.

MAIMONIDES

As long as Hanukkah is studied and remembered, Jews
will not surrender to the night. The proper response, as
Hanukkah teaches, is not to curse the darkness but to
light a candle.

IRVING GREENBERG

Just as Hanukkah candles are lighted one by one from a
single flame, so the tale of the miracle is passed from one
man to another, from one house to another, and to the
whole House of Israel throughout the generations.

JUDAH L. MAGNES

Is not Hanukkah a symbol of Israel,
and its light a symbol of his immortality?

LEO JUNG

Hanukkah is about the spark of the divine in all of us
made in God's image.

SUZANNE FIELDS

A candle is a small thing.
But one candle can light another.
And see how its own light increases,
as a candle gives its flame to the other.
You are such a light.

MOSHE DAVIS AND VICTOR RATNER

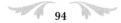

Kwanzaa

Kwanzaa is essentially a family holiday, whether it be
the nuclear family, the extended family, or the
communal family.

JESSICA B. HARRIS

Kwanzaa does not replace Christmas and is not a reli-
gious holiday. It is a time to focus on Africa and African-
inspired culture and to reinforce a value system that goes
back for generations.

ERIC V. COPAGE

The fact is that there is nowhere on the African continent a holiday named Kwanzaa.... Kwanzaa is an Afro-
American holiday which by its very definition reflects
the dual character of the identity and experience of the
Afro-American people.

MAULANA KARENGA

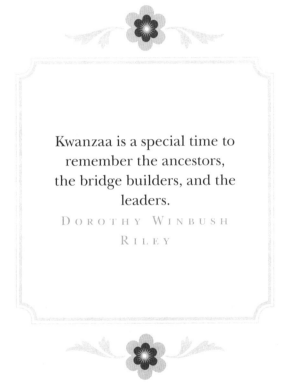

Kwanzaa is a special time to remember the ancestors, the bridge builders, and the leaders.

DOROTHY WINBUSH
RILEY

Like Christians at Christmas, African Americans now have a choice. They can ignore the inevitable commercialization of Kwanzaa and keep the home candles burning. Or they can celebrate Kwanzaa in the old-fashioned American way—by commodifying it.

KENNETH L. WOODWARD
AND PATRICE JOHNSON

Our children need the sense of specialness that comes from participating in a known and loved ritual.
They need the mastery of self-discipline that comes from order. They need the self-awareness that comes from a knowledge of their past.
They need Kwanzaa as a tool for building their future and our own.

JESSICA B. HARRIS

The ultimate destiny and aspiration
of the African people
and twenty million American Negroes are magnificently bound up together forever.

LORRAINE HANSBERRY

Kwanzaa affirms that mothers and fathers of previous generations transmitted African Americans' existence and persistence to the mothers and fathers of today. Pass it on.

DOROTHY WINBUSH RILEY

Let nothing and nobody break your spirit. Let the unity in the community remain intact.

JESSE JACKSON

The seven principles of Kwanzaa—unity, self-determination, collective work and responsibility, cooperative economics, purpose, creativity and faith—teach us that when we come together to strengthen our families and communities and honor the lesson of the past, we can face the future with joy and optimism.

BILL CLINTON

Celebrate
the Seasons

Summer

Summer afternoon—summer afternoon; to me those
have always been the two most beautiful words in the
English language.

HENRY JAMES

Summer is the time when one sheds one's tensions
with one's clothes, and the right kind of day is jeweled
balm for the battered spirit.
A few of those days and you can become
drunk with the belief that all's right with the world.

ADA LOUISE HUXTABLE

A perfect summer day is when the sun is shining,
the breeze is blowing, the birds are singing,
and the lawn mower is broken.

JAMES DENT

'Tis wealth enough of joy for me
In summer time to simply be.

PAUL LAURENCE DUNBAR

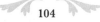

Rest is not idleness,
and to lie sometimes on the grass on
a summer day listening to the murmur of water, or
watching the clouds float across the sky,
is hardly a waste of time.

JOHN LUBBOCK

If a June night could talk,
it would probably boast that it invented romance.

BERN WILLIAMS

In June as many as a dozen species may burst their buds
on a single day. No man can heed all of these anniversaries; no man can ignore all of them.

ALDO LEOPOLD

I know of nothing that makes one feel
more complacent, in these July days,
than to have his vegetables from his own garden....
It is a kind of declaration of independence.

CHARLES DUDLEY WARNER

Of all the wonders of nature, a tree in summer is perhaps
the most remarkable, with the possible exception of a
moose singing "Embraceable You" in spats.

WOODY ALLEN

Summer is the topsy-turvy season when the goldfish have
to be boarded out while the family goes on a fishing trip.

ANONYMOUS

The bigger the summer vacation the harder the fall.

ANONYMOUS

When fortune empties her chamber pot on your head,
smile and say, "We are going to have a summer shower."

SIR JOHN A. MACDONALD

Do what we can, summer will have its flies.

RALPH WALDO EMERSON

Ah, summer, what power you have
to make us suffer and like it.

RUSSELL BAKER

Fall

Delicious autumn!
My very soul is wedded to it,
and if I were a bird
I would fly about the earth seeking
the successive autumns.

GEORGE ELIOT

No spring nor summer beauty hath such grace
As I have seen in one autumnal face.

JOHN DONNE

Autumn is a second spring
when every leaf is a flower.
ALBERT CAMUS

Thy bounty shines in autumn unconfined
And spreads a common feast for all that live.
JAMES THOMSON

Winter is an etching, spring a watercolor,
summer an oil painting
and autumn a mosaic of them all.
STANLEY HOROWITZ

Youth is like spring,
an over praised season more remarkable for
biting winds than genial breezes.
Autumn is the mellower season,
and what we lose in flowers
we more than gain in fruits.
SAMUEL BUTLER

Bittersweet October.
The mellow, messy, leaf-kicking, perfect pause between
the opposing miseries of summer and winter.
CAROL BISHOP HIPPS

The winds will blow their own freshness into you,
and the storms their energy, while cares will drop away
from you like the leaves of autumn.

JOHN MUIR

Everyone must take time to sit and watch the leaves turn.

ELIZABETH LAWRENCE

October's poplars are flaming torches
lighting the way to winter.

NOVA BAIR

Winter is what people go south during.

ANONYMOUS

Winter

There is this about a chill November:
It makes one appreciate a fireside.

HAL BORLAND

The cold was our pride,
the snow was our beauty.
It fell and fell,
lacing day and night together in a milky haze,
making everything quieter as it fell,
so that winter seemed to partake of religion
in a way no other season did,
hushed, solemn.

PATRICIA HAMPL

Turn down the noise. Reduce the speed.
Be like the somnolent
bears, or those other animals that slow down
and almost die in the
cold season. Let it be the way it is.
The magic is there in its power.

HENRY MITCHELL

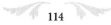

Winter, a lingering season,
is a time to gather golden moments,
embark upon a sentimental journey,
and enjoy every idle hour.

JOHN BOSWELL

There is a privacy
about it which no other season gives you….
In spring, summer and fall people sort of have an open
season on each other; only in the winter, in the country,
can you have longer, quiet stretches when you can savor
belonging to yourself.

RUTH STOUT

Winter is the time of promise
because there is so little to do—
or because you can now and then permit yourself
the luxury of thinking so.

STANLEY CRAWFORD

Winter is the time for comfort…
it is the time for home.

EDITH SITWELL

Green thoughts emerge from some deep source of still-
ness which the very fact of winter has released.

MIRABEL OSLER

I prefer winter and fall,
when you feel the bone structure in the landscape—
the loneliness of it—the dead feeling of winter.
Something waits beneath it—
the whole story doesn't show.

ANDREW WYETH

Every gardener knows that under the cloak of winter
lies a miracle: a seed waiting to sprout,
a bulb opening to the light,
a bud straining to unfurl.
And the anticipation nurtures our dream.

BARBARA WINKLER

There are two seasonal diversions that can ease the bite
of any winter. One is the January thaw.
The other is the seed catalogues.

HAL BORLAND

The flowers of late winter and early spring occupy places
in our hearts well out of proportion to their size.

GERTRUDE S. WISTER

In every winters' heart there is a quivering spring, and
behind the veil of each night there is a smiling dawn.

KAHLIL GIBRAN

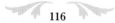

If we had no winter,
the spring would not
be so pleasant.

ANNE BRADSTREET

Spring

Winter is on my head, but eternal spring is in my heart.

VICTOR HUGO

No matter how long the winter, spring is sure to follow.

PROVERB

The nicest thing about the promise of spring
is that sooner or later she'll have to keep it.

MARK BELTAIRE

I stuck my head out the window this morning
and spring kissed me bang in the face.

LANGSTON HUGHES

Spring is when life's alive in everything.

CHRISTINA ROSSETTI

Spring is when you feel like whistling
even with a shoe full of slush.

DOUG LARSON

Spring shows what God can do
with a drab and dirty world.

VIRGIL A. KRAFT

April hath put a spirit of youth in everything.

WILLIAM SHAKESPEARE

April comes like an idiot, babbling, and strewing flowers.

EDNA ST. VINCENT MILLAY

The world's favorite season is the spring.
All things seem possible in May.

EDWIN WAY TEALE

Science has never drummed up quite as effective
a tranquilizing agent as a sunny spring day.

W. EARL HALL

I think that no matter how old or infirm I may become,
I will always plant a large garden in the spring. Who can
resist the feelings of hope and joy that one gets from
participating in nature's rebirth?

EDWARD GIOBBI

I love spring anywhere, but if I could choose
I would always greet it in a garden.

RUTH STOUT

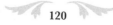

When the time is ripe for certain things, these things
appear in different places in the manner of violets
coming to light in the early spring.

FARKAS BOLYAI

Spring unlocks the flowers to paint the laughing soil.

REGINALD HEBER

Sweet spring, full of sweet days and roses,
a box where sweets compacted lie.

GEORGE HERBERT

Everything is blooming most recklessly; if it were voices
instead of colors, there would be an unbelievable
shrieking into the heart of the night.

RAINER MARIA RILKE

Sitting quietly, doing nothing,
Spring comes, and the grass
grows by itself.

ZEN SAYING

There is nothing like the first hot days of spring
when the gardener stops wondering
if it's too soon to plant the dahlias
and starts wondering if it's too late.

HENRY MITCHELL

Spring makes its own statement,
so loud and clear that the gardener seems to be
only one of the instruments, not the composer.

GEOFFREY B. CHARLESWORTH

If spring came but once a century
instead of once a year, or burst forth
with the sound of an earthquake and not in silence,
what wonder and expectation
there would be in all hearts
to behold the miraculous change.

HENRY WADSWORTH LONGFELLOW

Every spring is the only spring—
a perpetual astonishment.

ELLIS PETERS

Celebrate
Special People

Family

The family is one of nature's masterpieces.

GEORGE SANTAYANA

Realize that we are all members of one family.
We aren't members of different families.
Then each person is your mother, your father,
your sister, your brother.

MAHARAJ-JI

The family [is] the first essential cell of human society.

POPE JOHN XXIII

I don't care how poor a man is; if he has family, he's rich.

COLONEL POTTER, ON M*A*S*H

When you look at your life, the greatest
happinesses are family happinesses.

JOYCE BROTHERS

I know why families were created with all their imperfections. They humanize you. They are made to make you forget yourself occasionally, so that the beautiful balance of life is not destroyed.

ANAÏS NIN

Your family and your love must be cultivated like a garden. Time, effort, and imagination must be summoned constantly to keep any relationship flourishing and growing.

JIM ROHN

If you don't know [your family's] history, then you don't know anything. You are a leaf that doesn't know it is part of a tree.

MICHAEL CRICHTON

Family faces are magic mirrors. Looking at people who belong to us, we see the past, present, and future.

GAIL LUMET BUCKLEY

The debt of gratitude we owe
our mother and father
goes forward, not backward.
What we owe our parents
is the bill presented to us by
our children.

NANCY FRIDAY

He that has no fools, knaves, nor beggars in his family
was begot by a flash of lightning.

THOMAS FULLER

Family jokes, though rightly cursed by strangers,
are the bond that keeps most families alive.

STELLA BENSON

Ours is an old-fashioned family; my husband, the children, and I all have the same phone number.

JEAN H. MARVIN

Shared laughter is like family glue. It is the stuff of
family well-being and all-is-well thoughts. It brings us
together as few other things can.

VALERIE BELL

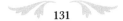

My family is really boring.
They have a coffee table book called
"Pictures We Took Just to Use Up the Rest of the Film."
PENELOPE LOMBARD

A family vacation is one where you arrive with five bags,
four kids and seven I-thought-you-packed-its.
IVERN BALL

Where can a person be better
than in the bosom of their family?
MARMONTEL GRETRY

Acting is just a way of making a living; the family is life.
DENZEL WASHINGTON

Perhaps the greatest social service
that can be rendered by anybody to this country
and to mankind is to bring up a family.
GEORGE BERNARD SHAW

You don't choose your family.
They are God's gift to you, as you are to them.
DESMOND TUTU

The family you come from isn't as important as the family
you're going to have.

RING LARDNER

Call it a clan, call it a network,
call it a tribe, call it a family.
Whatever you call it, whoever you are, you need one.

JANE HOWARD

Other things may change us
but we start and end with the family.

ANTHONY BRANDT

Children

Children are our most valuable natural resource.

HERBERT HOOVER

The soul is healed by being with children.

FYODOR DOSTOEVSKY

The best thing I've ever done?
Well, I've created four beautiful children.
You mean, other than that?

DONALD TRUMP

You can get children off your lap,
but you can never get them out of your heart.

ANONYMOUS

A child enters your home and for the next twenty years
makes so much noise you can hardly stand it. The child
departs, leaving the house so silent you think you are
going mad.

JOHN ANDREW HOLMES

My best creation
is my children.

DIANE VON
FÜRSTENBERG

What feeling is so nice as a child's hand in yours? So small, so soft and warm, like a kitten huddling in the shelter of your clasp.

MARJORIE HOLMES

Making the decision to have a child is momentous. It is to decide forever to have your heart go walking around outside your body.

ELIZABETH STONE

Babies are always more trouble than you thought— and more wonderful.

CHARLES OSGOOD

The only thing worth stealing is a kiss from a sleeping child.

JOE HOULDSWORTH

If my heart can become pure and simple like that of a child, I think there probably can be no greater happiness than this.

KITARO NISHIDA

Children, one earthly Thing truly experienced, even
once, is enough for a lifetime.

RAINER MARIA RILKE

To bring up a child in a way he should go,
travel that way yourself once in a while.

JOSH BILLINGS

You should study not only that you
become a mother when your child is born,
but also that you become a child.

DOGEN

Stay close to the young and a little rubs off.

ALAN JAY LERNER

You can learn many things from children.
How much patience you have, for instance.

FRANKLIN P. JONES

A three-year-old child is a being who gets almost as much
fun out of a fifty-six dollar set of swings as it does
out of finding a small green worm.

BILL VAUGHAN

It now costs more to amuse a child
than it once did to educate his father.

VAUGHN MONROE

It would seem that something which means poverty,
disorder and violence every single day
should be avoided entirely, but the desire
to beget children is a natural urge.

PHYLLIS DILLER

There are two lasting bequests we can give our children:
One is roots. The other is wings.

HODDING CARTER, JR.

A mother always has to think
twice, once for herself and
once for her child.

SOPHIA LOREN

Children have never been good at listening to their
elders, but they have never failed to imitate them.

JAMES BALDWIN

Children may close their ears to advice,
but open their eyes to example.

ANONYMOUS

If you want your children to improve, let them overhear
the nice things you say about them to others.

HAIM GINOTT

Kids learn more from example than anything you say.
I'm convinced they learn very early not to hear anything
you say, but watch what you do.

JANE PAULEY

The best inheritance a parent can give to his children
is a few minutes of their time each day.

ORLANDO A. BATTISTA

Likely as not, the child you can do the least with
will do the most to make you proud.

MIGNON MCLAUGHLIN

The darn trouble with cleaning the house is it gets dirty
the next day anyway, so skip a week if you have to.
The children are the most important thing.

BARBARA BUSH

Cleaning your house while your kids are still growing
is like shoveling the walk before it stops snowing.

PHYLLIS DILLER

Human beings are the only creatures on earth
that allow their children to come back home.

BILL COSBY

The way to keep children at home is to make home a
pleasant atmosphere—and to let the air out of the tires.

DOROTHY PARKER

It kills you to see them grow up.
But I guess it would kill you quicker if they didn't.

BARBARA KINGSOLVER

Few things are more satisfying than seeing your children
have teenagers of their own.

DOUG LARSON

There are two things a child will share willingly—
communicable diseases and his mother's age.

BENJAMIN SPOCK

Life affords no greater responsibility, no great privilege,
than the raising of the next generation.

C. EVERETT KOOP

In every child who is born, under no matter what circum-
stances, and of no matter what parents,
the potentiality of the human race is born again.

JAMES AGEE

Children are a great comfort in your old age,
and they help you reach it faster, too.

LIONEL KAUFFMAN

Few things are more delightful than grandchildren
fighting over your lap.

DOUG LARSON

The birth of a grandchild
is a wonderful and exciting event! That wonder and
excitement continues throughout life.

TOM POTTS

When a child is born, so are grandmothers.

JUDITH LEVY

By the time the youngest children have learned to keep
the house tidy, the oldest grandchildren are on hand to
tear it to pieces.

CHRISTOPHER MORLEY

Never have children, only grandchildren.

GORE VIDAL

Grandparents

Nobody can do for little children what grandparents do.
Grandparents sort of sprinkle stardust over the lives of
little children.

ALEX HALEY

If I really begged her, Nanny would take her teeth out
and smile at me. I never saw anything so funny in my life.

CAROL BURNETT

I loved their home.
Everything smelled older, worn but safe;
the food aroma had baked itself into the furniture.

SUSAN STRASBERG

Becoming a grandparent is a second chance.
For you have a chance
to put to use all the things you learned
the first time around
and may have made mistakes on.
It's all love and no discipline.
There's no thorn in the rose.

JOYCE BROTHERS

The simplest toy,
one which even the youngest
child can operate,
is called a grandparent.

SAM LEVENSON

To reform a man, you must begin with his grandmother.

VICTOR HUGO

Grandchildren don't make a man feel old; it's the knowledge that he's married to a grandmother.

G. NORMAN COLLIE

Grandmas are moms with lots of frosting.

ANONYMOUS

If your baby "is beautiful and perfect, never cries or fusses, sleeps on schedule and burps on demand, is an angel all the time"... you're the grandma.

TERESA BLOOMINGDALE

Becoming a grandmother is wonderful. One moment you're just a mother. The next you are all-wise and prehistoric.

PAM BROWN

A mother becomes a true grandmother the day she stops
noticing the terrible things her children do because she
is too enchanted with the wonderful things her grandchildren do.

LOIS WYSE

I'm not a picture-toting grandma—
but my grandsons, Tyler J. Phillips
and Dean Phillips, just happen to be the best-looking,
smartest, best-mannered grandchildren
in the continental United States—
and you can throw in Canada and the Virgin Islands.

ABIGAIL VAN BUREN

I never thought she'd turn on me. When I was sinking in
a sea of diapers, formulas, and congenital spitting,
Mother couldn't wait to pull her grandchildren onto her
lap and say, "Let me tell you how rotten your mommy
was. She never took naps, and she never picked up her
room, and she has a mouth like a drunken
sailor in Shanghai. I washed her mouth out with soap so
many times I finally had to starch her tongue."

ERMA BOMBECK

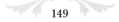

Grandmotherhood does not give us the right to speak without thinking, but only the right to think without speaking.

LOIS WYSE

Grandma was a kind of first-aid station,
or a Red Cross nurse,
who took up where the battle ended,
accepting us and our little
sobbing sins, gathering the whole of us into her lap,
restoring us to health and confidence by her amazing
faith in life and in a mortal's strength to meet it.

LILLIAN SMITH

If you want to know where I come by the passionate commitment I have to bringing people together without regard to race, it all started with my grandfather.

BILL CLINTON

My grandfather once told me that there were two kinds of people: those who do the work and those who take the credit. He told me to try to be in the first group; there was much less competition.

INDIRA GANDHI

Grandfather was well known
for being stubborn in his
ideas. For instance...you had
to go to sleep facing east
so that you would be ready
to greet the sun when it
returned.

MICHAEL DORRIS

Holding a great-grandchild
makes getting old worthwhile.

EVALYN RIKKERS

The closest friends I have made all through life
have been people who also grew up close to a loved and
living grandmother or grandfather.

MARGARET MEAD

It's funny what happens when you become a grandparent.
You start to act all goofy and do things you never
thought you'd do. It's terrific.

MIKE KRZYZEWSKI

My grandfather's a little forgetful, but he likes to give me
advice. One day, he took me aside and left me there.

RON RICHARDS

If nothing is going well, call your grandmother.

ITALIAN PROVERB

Friends

Celebrate the happiness that friends are always giving,
make every day a holiday and celebrate just living!

AMANDA BRADLEY

Gems may be precious, but friends are priceless.

ANONYMOUS

My friends are my estate.

EMILY DICKINSON

A friend is a gift you give yourself.

ROBERT LOUIS STEVENSON

A friend might well be reckoned
the masterpiece of nature.

RALPH WALDO EMERSON

I can trust my friends. These people force me
to examine, encourage me to grow.

CHER

My best friend is the one who brings out the best in me.

HENRY FORD

When friends stop being frank and useful to each other,
the whole world loses some of its radiance.

ANATOLE BROYARD

No man is the whole of himself.
His friends are the rest of him.

PROVERB

In my friend, I find a second self.

ISABEL NORTON

Each friend represents a world in us, a world possibly not
born until they arrive, and it is only by this meeting that
a new world is born.

ANAÏS NIN

Treat your friends as you do your pictures,
and place them in their best light.

JENNIE JEROME CHURCHILL

Lots of people want to ride
with you in the limo, but what
you want is someone who will
take the bus with you when
the limo breaks down.

OPRAH WINFREY

The true friend is the one that's coming in the door
while everyone else is going out.

PHIL MCGRAW

A good friend—like a tube of toothpaste—
comes through in a tight squeeze.

ANONYMOUS

If a friend is in trouble, don't annoy him by asking if
there is anything you can do. Think up something appro-
priate and do it.

EDGAR WATSON HOWE

It is the friends that you can call at 4 A.M. that matter.

MARLENE DIETRICH

Everyone hears what you say.
Friends listen to what you say.
Best friends listen to what you don't say.

ANONYMOUS

Nothing makes the earth seem so spacious
as to have friends at a distance:
they make the latitudes and longitudes.

HENRY DAVID THOREAU

Go oft to the house of thy friend,
for weeds choke the unused path.

RALPH WALDO EMERSON

If two friends ask you to judge a dispute, don't accept,
because you will lose one friend; on the other hand,
if two strangers come with the same request, accept
because you will gain one friend.

SAINT AUGUSTINE

Before borrowing money from a friend,
decide which you need the most.

AMERICAN PROVERB

True friendship is like sound health;
the value of it is seldom known until it be lost.

CHARLES CALEB COLTON

The best way to keep your friends
is not to give them away.

WILSON MIZNER

"Are we going to be friends forever?" asked Piglet.
"Even longer," Pooh answered.

A. A. MILNE, WINNIE THE POOH

To find a friend one must close one eye—
to keep him, two.

NORMAN DOUGLAS

A true friend is one who overlooks your failures
and tolerates your successes.

DOUG LARSON

A friend is someone
who makes me feel totally acceptable.

ENE RIISNA

A friend is someone who sees through you
and still enjoys the view.

WILMA ASKINAS

A friend is one who knows all about you
and likes you anyway.

CHRISTI MARY WARNER

Friendship is one mind in two bodies.

MENCIUS

Misfortune shows those who are not really friends.

ARISTOTLE

The friendship that can cease has never been real.

SAINT JEROME

Don't walk in front of me, I may not follow.
Don't walk behind me, I may not lead.
Walk beside me and be my friend.

ALBERT CAMUS

The best thing to do behind a friend's back is pat it.

RUTH BRILLHART

Our job is not to straighten each other out,
but to help each other up.

NEVA COLE

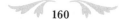

160

It is a good thing to be rich, it
is a good thing to be strong,
but it is a better thing to be
beloved by many friends.

EURIPIDES

He who has a thousand friends has not a friend to spare,
and he who has one enemy will meet him everywhere.

RALPH WALDO EMERSON

God gives us our relatives;
thank God we can choose our friends!

ETHEL WATTS MUMFORD

One loyal friend
is better than ten thousand family members.

ANONYMOUS

The making of friends, who are real friends,
is the best token we have of a man's success in life.

EDWARD EVERETT HALE

My father always used to say that when you die,
if you've got five real friends, you've had a great life.

LEE IACOCCA

A life without a friend is a life without sun.

GERMAN PROVERB

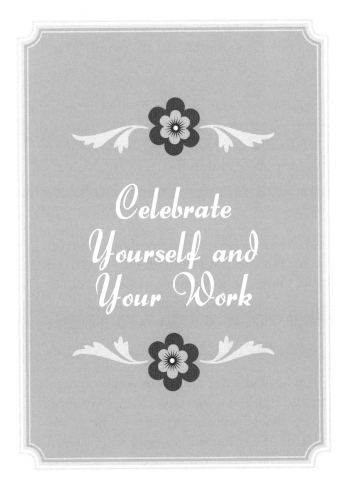

Celebrate
Yourself and
Your Work

We are cups, constantly and quietly being filled.
The trick is knowing
how to tip ourselves over and let the beautiful stuff out.

RAY BRADBURY

Men go abroad to wonder at the heights of mountains,
at the huge waves of the sea, at the long courses of the
rivers, at the vast compass of the ocean, at the circular
motions of the stars, and they pass by themselves without
wondering.

SAINT AUGUSTINE

Nature always gets credit which should in truth be
reserved for ourselves: the rose for its scent; the nightingale for its song; and the sun for its radiance. The poets
are entirely mistaken.
They should address their lyrics to themselves.

ALFRED NORTH WHITEHEAD

You have to leave the city of your comfort
and go into the wilderness of your intuition.
What you will discover will be
wonderful. What you will discover will be yourself.

ALAN ALDA

The potential of the average person
is like a huge ocean unsailed, a new continent
unexplored, a world of possibilities waiting
to be released and channeled toward some great good.

BRIAN TRACY

The race advances only by the extra achievements
of the individual. You are the individual.

CHARLES TOWNE

Most people have no idea of the giant capacity we can
immediately command when we focus all our resources
on a single area of our lives.

ANTHONY ROBBINS

Cherish your visions and your dreams,
as they are the children of your soul;
the blueprints of your ultimate achievements.

NAPOLEON HILL

All the wonders you seek are
within yourself.

SIR THOMAS BROWN

The only thing that will stop you
from fulfilling your dreams is you.

TOM BRADLEY

It is never too late to be what you might have been.

GEORGE ELIOT

People often say that this or that person has not yet
found himself. But the self is not something one finds, it
is something one creates.

THOMAS SZASZ

Catch on fire with enthusiasm
and people will come for miles
to watch you burn.

JOHN WESLEY

If you think you're too small to make a difference,
you haven't been in bed with a mosquito.

ANITA RODDICK

We are each gifted in a unique and important way. It
is our privilege and our adventure to discover our own
special light.

MARY DUNBAR

We are all worms, but I do believe I am a glowworm.

WINSTON CHURCHILL

The first love affair we need to consummate successfully
is with ourselves, because only then will we
be ready for relationships with others.

NATHANIEL BRANDEN

When one is out of touch with oneself,
one cannot touch others.

ANNE MORROW LINDBERGH

In the depth of winter
I finally learned that there was in me
an invincible summer.

ALBERT CAMUS

We have to learn to be our own best friends because we
fall too easily into the trap of being our worst enemies.

RODERICK THORP

One's self-image is very important because
if that's in good shape, then you can do anything,
or practically anything.

SIR JOHN GIELGUD

The better we feel about ourselves, the fewer times we
have to knock somebody else down to feel tall.

ODETTA

A human being's first responsibility
is to shake hands with himself.

HENRY WINKLER

Friendship with oneself is all important,
because without it one cannot be friends
with anyone else in the world.

ELEANOR ROOSEVELT

He who knows others is learned;
he who knows himself is wise.

LAO-TZU

The ultimate lesson all of us have to learn
is unconditional love,
which includes not only others
but ourselves as well.

ELISABETH KÜBLER-ROSS

Learn to enjoy your own
company. You are the one
person you can count on
living with for the
rest of your life.

ANN RICHARDS

To love oneself is the beginning of a lifelong romance.
OSCAR WILDE

I never loved another person the way I loved myself.
MAE WEST

Self-love is the greatest of all flatterers.
FRANÇOIS, DUC DE LA ROCHEFOUCAULD

At bottom every man knows perfectly well
that he is a unique being, only once on this earth;
and by no extraordinary chance
will such a marvelously picturesque piece of diversity
in unity as he is,
ever be put together a second time.
FRIEDRICH NIETZSCHE

If I try to be like him, who will be like me?
YIDDISH PROVERB

You don't get harmony
when everybody sings the same note.
DOUG FLOYD

When there is an original sound in the world,
it wakens a hundred echoes.

JOHN A. SHEDD

All I would tell people is to hold onto what was individual
about themselves, not to allow their ambition for success
to cause them to try to imitate the success of others.
You've got to find it on your own terms.

HARRISON FORD

Let me listen to me and not to them.

GERTRUDE STEIN

Don't accept that others know you better than yourself.

SONJA FRIEDMAN

Your only obligation in any lifetime
is to be true to yourself.

RICHARD BACH

Know yourself. Don't accept your dog's admiration
as conclusive evidence that you are wonderful.

ANN LANDERS

Resolve to be thyself;
and know that he who finds himself, loses his misery.

MATTHEW ARNOLD

You've got to do your own growing,
no matter how tall your grandfather was.

IRISH PROVERB

We are the hero of our own story.

MARY McCARTHY

Do not rely completely on any other human being,
however dear.
We meet all life's greatest tests alone.

AGNES CAMPBELL MACPHAIL

Seek out that particular mental attribute which makes
you feel most deeply and vitally alive, along with which
comes the inner voice which says, "This is the real me,"
and when you have found that attitude, follow it.

JAMES TRUSLOW ADAMS

There are no menial jobs,
only menial attitudes.

WILLIAM J. BENNETT

If a man is called to be a street sweeper,
he should sweep streets even as Michelangelo painted,
or Beethoven played music,
or Shakespeare wrote poetry.
He should sweep streets so well that all the hosts of
heaven and earth will pause to say, here lived a great
street sweeper who did his job well.

MARTIN LUTHER KING, JR.

What you do is more important than
how much you make, and how you feel about it
is more important than what you do.

JERRY GILLIES

There's no labor a man can do that's undignified—
if he does it right.

BILL COSBY

My father always told me, "Find a job you love
and you'll never have to work a day in your life."

JIM FOX

Work and play are words used to describe
the same thing under differing conditions.

MARK TWAIN

The more I want to get something done,
the less I call it work.

RICHARD BACH

Are you bored with life?
Then throw yourself into some work
you believe in with all your heart,
live for it, die for it,
and you will find happiness
that you had thought could never be yours.

DALE CARNEGIE

In every community, there is work to be done.
In every nation, there are wounds to heal.
In every heart, there is the power to do it.

MARIANNE WILLIAMSON

In order that people may be happy in their work,
these three things are needed:
they must be fit for it; they must not do too much of it;
and they must have a sense of success in it.

JOHN RUSKIN

Look at a day when you are
supremely satisfied at the end.
It's not a day when you lounge around doing nothing.
It's when you've had everything to do,
and you've done it.

MARGARET THATCHER

Never continue in a job you don't enjoy.
If you're happy in what
you're doing, you'll like yourself,
you'll have inner peace. And if you
have that, along with physical health,
you will have had more success
than you could possibly have imagined.

RODAN OF ALEXANDRIA

Doing what we were meant to do creates fun, excitement and contentment in our lives, and invariably, in the lives of the people around us. When you're excited about something it's contagious.

MARK VICTOR HANSEN

The work of the individual still remains the spark that moves mankind forward.

IGOR SIKORSKY

We have only this moment,
sparkling like a star
in our hand…
and melting like a snowflake.
Let us use it
before it is too late.

MARIE BEYNON RAY

INDEX TO AUTHORS

Allen Klein is an award-winning professional speaker and bestselling author. His first book, *The Healing Power of Humor*, which is now in a thirty-eighth printing and ninth foreign language translation, perfectly sums up his life-long philosophy—that humor is the best medicine for all ailments, big and small. A recipient of a Lifetime Achievement Award from the Association for Applied and Therapeutic Humor and an inductee into the Hunter College, New York City, Hall of Fame, Allen is also the world's only certified Jollytologist®, earning a Master's Degree from St. Mary's College in humor—no kidding! Nicknamed the "King of Whimsy," Allen has even worked in television production, designing children's shows at CBS, including the beloved and wildly popular *Captain Kangaroo*. The author of seventeen uplifting and inspiring books, Allen currently resides and writes in San Francisco.

For more information about his books and presentations, go to www.allenklein.com or contact him at allen@allenklein.com